CW00832102

ISBN: 978-0-9956320-0-4

Published in 2017 by Structo Press
www.structopress.co.uk
Typeset in Perpetua by Euan Monaghan

Cover art by David Russomano

ACKNOWLEDGEMENTS

'Two Coincidences', 'Writing Home from Quepos' and 'After the Revolution:
Katmandu, 2006': *Obsessed with Pipework* 67
'Phonsavanh' and 'Twister': *Verse-Virtual* Vol. 3 No. 1
'We Pass': *Reaping* (Inwood Indiana, 2016)
'What Begins and Ends with Water or June, 2015': *Seethingography* June 2016
'Ankara': *Cahoodaloodaling* 15
'Murmuration': *Impressment Gang* Vol. 3 No. 2

THANK YOU

Jane Yeh, Martha Sprackland, Todd Swift, Michael Sarnowski, Lucy Furlong,
and everyone else who offered editorial guidance and encouragement along
the way, especially my wife.

Contents

Two Coincidences

I.

In towns about an hour east of New York
and thirty minutes south of London:
feral parakeets (Monk and Rose-ringed)
barrel past with a chorus of squawks,
scattering like neon green buckshot.
When we meet, in East Java of all places,
(though it takes us two and a half years
to notice) these invasive species
are among the things we have in common.

II.

After two sons
and one daughter,
for nothing more
than symmetry's sake,
my parents, sure
that they'd swaddle
another child in pink,
were ready
to give me what,
thirty years later,
would turn out to be
my wife's first
and middle names.

We Pass

gas stations, grain silos, a small cemetery,
telephone poles marching single file,

mills, a bowling alley, fast food chains
with names that we all recognize,

a maze carved into a corn field, red barns
protected by Pennsylvania Dutch hex signs,

homes, over-populated parking lots, a pickup truck
flying a miniature flag from its tailgate,

two-tone cows, West Main Street,
imperative slogans telling us which cola to drink,

roadside attractions (a railroad museum
and the oldest turkey farm in the nation),

a placard advertising real estate,
saying *Rental and Sales* on one side

with *NO WAR NO WAR* on the other
in a black scrawl that looks like it's dripping.

Writing Home from Quepos

The flipped light switch sends a cockroach running for cover down my shower drain. This is the way days start here, but I don't mention it so you won't worry. When I describe the old shop owner next door, the way he answers every *Cómo está* with *Pura vida*, I leave out the part about his missing leg though, as far as I'm concerned, that's the whole point of the story. Instead, I tell you how those boats seem calm on the grey Pacific; how a pickup truck passes, heavy with pineapples; how one of the town's churches grows another story, how it wears the scaffolding like some kind of crown. If I tell you that the laundry isn't opened on Sundays, you might appreciate their respect for the Sabbath, but you're just as likely to fret about me running out of clean clothes, so I skip it. I want to help you imagine the town—corner cantinas, quiet till dusk; ticos lounging in Sodas, watching their teams on TVs beside Coca-Cola coolers; ticas shunning strollers, holding babies closer; girls riding side-saddle on their boyfriend's bicycles. You'd rather hear about exotic animals. So I tell you about the squirrel monkeys performing tree-branch trapeze acts and power-line acrobatics; about the time I saw one chased out of the canopy by a black howler twice its size, desperately outmatched but still chirping for a fight. I tell you about tiny geckos clinging to my windows, waiting for flies; about enormous iguanas lumbering into the trees across the street like something out of prehistory; about the lizards no one else notices basking on boulders around the harbour and the way I'm getting better at spotting their small black eyes. But there's a rain-shaped hole in all of this and, without warning, it starts to seep in. It's there at dinner in the café during the Andean pan pipe cover of 'Dust in the Wind'. It's weighing down palm fronds and beating steel roofs. It's the crippled umbrellas wallowing in puddles. It's everything abrasive. It's the vultures in the mud at low tide; it's the filthy decal of Christ's face on the bumper of a bus; it's concrete punctuated by blood from a dog fight or something grimmer; it's the man asleep on the sidewalk with a flattened cardboard box for a mattress and the woman a few feet away sweeping dust off her gated porch, locked behind its bars; it's the mad lady pacing through the bus station while I'm waiting to leave; the way she's yelling *adiós* over and over; the way that even I've stopped listening.

On Leoni Bridge

A canal sixty years in length
runs from the city of bridges
to an unmarked London grave.

Midway, where the flow coincides
with Carshalton Park, a commission
is stillborn—drafted and scrapped—

save this Palladian arrangement
of white Portland stone.
It still spans the River Wandle

like a subdued cringe crossing
the Venetian's face when patrons
anglicised Giacomo to James.

Rudy's

Scanning all the names and phrases carved right
into the wooden walls and tables, I
absently trace each of the gouged letters,
but double vision blurs them together.

Behind the bar, the oversized mirror
wearing a whiskey's name makes me wonder
what the looking glass and liquor could share.
Both give the feeling of doubling what's there.

While I mull this over, lit beer logos
cast nets of neon through the front windows.
The persuasive glow draws customers in
like bug zappers do. *No coincidence*

we're called barflies, I think aloud and laugh,
drinking, then catching myself in the glass.

After the Revolution: Kathmandu, 2006

I.

the sacred pond in Bhaktapur
where the vendors and guides agree
that tossing an oh-so-affordable handful
of brightly coloured rice balls to the carp
is lucky—the way that fish as thick
as my thigh emerge from the murk,
frenzied, piling up on each other's backs,
a roiling mass conditioned to chase
every scrap they're tossed, driven
out of their element, choking on air

II.

the street corner shrine in Patan
housing a stone Ganesh so worn down
by the pestle of years and the caress
of countless reverent hands applying
powdered saffron that the smudge
of his face is nearly featureless when
a teenage girl in a Pink Floyd T-shirt
rubs brilliant prayer on what's left
of his trunk and I try to guess what
obstacle she wants removed from her path

III.

the ghats beside Pashupatinath
where, in the rain, my guide encourages
me to capture an inconsolable family
stoking their pyre and, though I refuse
to shoot the relatives—seemingly crushed

in giant fists of grief—or the smouldering
remains, when I photograph the orderly row
of Shaivite shrines standing to attention
on the opposite bank, the smoke
snakes its way into the frame

Reflections

I scoffed when they claimed he'd found it, called it
unsubstantiated gossip, and muttered
'wild goose chase', albeit with less conviction,
when he furnished charts and coordinates.

He *was* different, healthier, more vigorous.
Still, only after droves of subsequent sippers
brought back whispers of limited supply
and second chances did I shamble onto deck,

gambling on pilgrimage's salty sails. For weeks,
I waited on my knees, in sickness and in prayer
while cloud and wave competed for the prize
of blackest threat. Landfall would've been a boon,

if not for the tangled swamps' suck and sting.
Unflagging, I pushed on and finally found
the infamous font drained, its defunct spouts blocked
by clumps of moss, coins strewn across its basin

sheathed in green. Because the shallow murk offered
naught save my stagnant reflection, I ruptured that face
with a silver wish and began the long retreat,
but sprang back before the splash could settle,

lapping up the noxious puddle like a mutt.
It smelt of gutter. It couldn't have been sweeter.

St. John's

The cemetery on the hill closed at dusk,
so when the cop pulled up behind my car
I was technically trespassing, and I don't
blame him for thinking I might have been
there to smoke pot or kick over headstones,
but I only ever visited the highest point
in my hometown for the quiet I found
between those rows of marble and granite.

There's nothing for privacy like a graveyard
after dark, unless it's tainted by some
slack-jawed dick with a flashlight
and a homicide, recounted nonchalantly
while looking over your license: 'One guy
bashed another guy's brains in, right here,
thirteen years ago. Love triangle.
Actually, I knew all three of them.'

Murmuration

Dip the stiff brush into Mars Black and again

> *Through the window of a Turkish bus, driving*

into a transparent glass. In the clouds, tight

> *over the Anatolian plains at dusk, watch*

wisps of pigment drink and relax—dark, dancing—

> *a ribbon of starlings unfurled, their dip and turn,*

impossibly smooth, as if to unheard music.

> *a whirling couple, quick heels and billowing dress.*

Cutting Corners

The brake pad factory's Superfund signature:
an indelible black smudge of asbestos,
PCBs, and lead far too costly
to ever completely erase—
just swept under the asphalt carpet
of a fresh shopping complex
and the heels of the bargain conscious.

On frigid afternoons, in years sandwiched
between carcinogens and discounts,
when our doughnut town framed
the desolate hole of that lot, the path
of least resistance from Stratford High
to Graf-Wadman's second-hand CD selection
meant furtive trespass through vacancy.
In an inch of snow, mid-trudge, we paused, spun,
and boggled at how vast it was, or just seemed.

More than a decade after graduation,
after superstores and hordes of cars
filled that space in, after the music shop
called it quits and we moved away
in opposite directions, I'm still hung up
on the cold hush of that expansiveness
where almost nothing could touch us.

What Begins and Ends with Water

or

June, 2015

1st
a municipal tanker truck's hose
douses flower baskets
hanging from high street lamp posts,
the excess pouring onto pavement,
channelled along cracks and seams,
pooling in the most deeply damaged places;
in the morning, on the way to work,
stepping over these

13th
milling around outside the venue
under a tarnished sky
between the ceremony and reception,
sporadic droplets and soured light
harry the guests and photographer
but have no effect on the smiles
of the groom or bride

16th
before, during, and after
the heart attack, his shower head
fulfills its function, water delivered
through a constellation of holes
as always, rinsing him upright,
doubled over, collapsed,
the flow still cleansing, washing,
then washing away

30th
easel poised on Kingston Bridge
as the day ends, face to the Thames,
back turned on traffic, a painter
wielding canvas, brushes, and palette
like fly paper, trying to catch,
intact, what never ceases,
reaching for everything
that's slipping beneath him

Here on Business?

after 'Watching the Storm (Denver)' by John Register

Between meeting's end and evening meal,
a late afternoon lull settles into the room
like long-haul creases in a pristine suit.

Some TV, an airport paperback, staring up
at hairline ceiling cracks—he's exhausted
all of his finest tools for whittling away

at time, besides calling his wife and kids.
He pushes beige curtains aside and points a chair
towards Denver's skyline: a row of blank glass

high rises behind squat brick apartment blocks with
parking lots dominating the foreground.
He tries to count hatchbacks, station wagons, sedans,

and souped-up coupes, but his mind's already
absconded ten floors down, imagining order,
trite bartender chit chat, and the golden

moment he finally gets hold of his distraction—
the kind of refrain that's stuck in your head
unless you go and listen to the song again.

In the distance, there's a storm moving in.
Even before he turns and leaves that seat vacant
in a clean wedge of light, he can't see it.

Phonsavan

The plain studded with megalithic jars,
vessels so large that legend has them dropped
from giants' hands, discarded at the end
of their last enormous party. Stone grey
against green, these ancient cups lie scattered
like cluster munitions, ruptured and tipped
by trees, paused in the posture of spilling.
This is what we come to see, though our tour
includes visits to more recent relics
(a matter of secondary targets):
what's left of a Russian tank, rust bucket,
every loose piece prised off and sold for scrap;
that blackened cave where unarmed hundreds hid
until it swallowed a U.S. rocket;
and craters persisting in rice paddies
like the circular battle scars squids leave
on sperm whales as they wrestle in darkness.

(Reasons for) Moving

It's the ice cream van that circles our block,
looping a tinny jingle with one bent note.

It's the breezy park where granola bar wrappers
twirl like jewellery box ballerinas.

It's the train trestle housing so many pigeons
that it casts a sort of off-white shadow.

It's the evening rain that coaxes snails
out under the heels of morning commuters.

It's the neighbour's skip across from us
where a fox settles in to sleep on the rubbish.

It's the vapour trails from Heathrow and Gatwick
hanging overhead like a net's entrapment.

It's the waves of gulls that head west at dusk
as if they're escaping from something together.

On Discovering a Page of Newsprint Tucked into a Second-hand Book about Easter Island

February 9th, 1959
(according to the New York Herald Tribune,
page 5): just ahead of Valentine's,
they're selling gentlemen's hats
and heart-shaped boxes of perfume.

Chinatown has hatched
the Year of the Boar. The POHS Institute
is offering a real estate course.
Thurgood Marshall's questioning the pace
of desegregation in schools.

The U.S. has incontrovertible proof
that Soviets shot down their transport plane
(Moscow insists that it's fake).
The New York Authority wants more power
to generate power, no matter

how many Tuscarora Indians
stand in their way. For a limited time,
B. Altman & Co. has great deals
on sofa slip covers, made-to-order.
Between reports of Cuban firing squads

and an ad for non-stop European flights
with Royal Dutch Airlines: a 50 word piece
about a 75 year old's suicide. Name, address,
how his brother found him pyjama-clad, hanging
in the bathroom of his 19th floor apartment.

Twister

Match the white Bengal tiger's gaze,
his eyes the blue of frosted glass
and front paws broader than your chest,
with no more than a splinter of thought
for what one quick gesture could do.
Now, instead of that dull New Jersey zoo,
picture meeting in the Sunderbans' green
with the assurance of fences removed.

This is the way it feels to watch
the clouds drop a rope into the sea,
tethering one grey to another—with
so little between matchstick bungalows
and the water spout's ferocity—
too tangled in fear to breathe until
the taut cord snaps just offshore,
its ends unravelling above and below.

At Play on Phnom Bakheng

Watching, you could guess the rules—
take a desiccated military-green seed pod
split down its seam into oblong halves;
hold in small hands;
toss against the breeze;
let it open, falling into red dust
with both faces up, down, or one of each;
win, lose, repeat.

Perched on the crippled summit of a mountain
made to mimic heaven in stone,
two Khmer girls play with the pieces,
taking it in turn among the crowds' feet,
while foreign lenses strain
through rippled heat for a sunset
caught on Angkor Wat
like all the guide books said it would be.

Haunting

February, 1895: once Gardner Lake
is solid enough to uphold ice skaters,
a crew raises Thomas LeCount's house onto sleds
and begins to inch it across. Dead set on finding
an easier way to move than having his whole home
broken down and pieced back together, this is the best
shortcut that he can come up with. The rest plays out
as if scripted—a hundred yards in, an errant snow drift
brings it all off the skids. Between this debacle
and nightfall, they agree it can wait until morning.
         The proverbial rude awakening—
back rooms submerged, porch at an obscene angle.
They salvage everything small enough to haul out,
but surrender the most unwieldy pieces:
a cast iron stove, the family piano. Even now,
it's down there with the walleye and catfish.
Though no one dies in it, you'll find this bound up
with the other ghost stories of Connecticut.
Locals say that if you take a boat out after dark
and wait over what's left of the roof, you'll hear
a hollow melody surfacing like bubbles.

Ankara

For two years
the muezzin's song
was our lullaby
and wakeup call—

familiar like the aroma
of yoğurt çorbası,
never a favourite,
though we had it often.

The recitation
poured from minarets,
purring between
stark apartment blocks

like a housecat
doing warm figure eights
tight against
its owner's shins.

Even now, a kernel
of melody persists,
suggesting a silence
we'd never known was there,

like the patch of wall
you find behind a painting,
the only spot
that the sun hasn't faded.

Notes on the text

'Writing Home from Quepos' refers to a town in western Costa Rica. 'Pura vida' is Costa Rican slang, which literally means 'pure life', though a combination of 'no worries' and 'it's all good' would be a more accurate translation. 'Ticos' and 'ticas' are guys and girls.

'On Leoni Bridge' refers to Giacomo Leoni, an Italian architect who had a significant impact on British design in the early 18th century.

'Rudy's' refers to a bar in New Haven, Connecticut, which has since changed its name. The original owners of Rudy's opened another bar of the same name elsewhere in New Haven.

'After the Revolution: Kathmandu, 2006' refers to the period immediately following May 18th, 2006, when Nepal, the world's only Hindu Kingdom, was officially declared a secular country.

'Cutting Corners' refers to Superfund, an American governmental program dealing with sites contaminated by toxic substances. Graf-Wadman was a record store in Connecticut.

'Here on Business?' refers to the work of the 20th century American realist painter John Register. For more information, see *John Register: Persistent Observer* by Barnaby Conrad III.